The Honey Spout

"Stay under the spout from where the honey flows out!"

by

Bruce Everhart Sr.

authorHOUSE®

AuthorHouse™
1663 Liberty Drive, Suite 200
Bloomington, IN 47403
www.authorhouse.com
Phone: 1-800-839-8640

First published by AuthorHouse 6/28/2007

ISBN: 978-1-4343-1660-8 (sc)

Library of Congress Control Number: 2007903770

Printed in the United States of America
Bloomington, Indiana

This book is printed on acid-free paper.

Introduction

Dear friends I am not writing this book because of some wild idea. I am writing it out of 38 years of experience of mistakes I have made, of being denied by fellow Christians, putdown and called a devil, forced out of churches with no one to go to for counseling. I had to stand on God's word that he would never leave me or forsake me and study my Bible to know what Gods word had promised me and believe God could somehow finish what he had started in my life. And guess what; he has never failed me when I went to him for help and he will never fail you if you are sincere. Maybe he will not answer you the way you want him to but he will answer you in his way and in his time, the best way. His ways are higher in the heavens than our ways. I have lived both sides of this life and I have found out that this Christ side is the best side.

I am writing this book out of my heart, the things I am putting in this book have been in my heart for a number of years. I have been praying for God to make a way for me to get them out to other people. My thoughts have been, God why have you taught me all these things and I can not seem to get them out. I have been trying for about two years to no avail. Maybe just maybe this is the way. You see folks I never dreamed of ever writing a book. I have never even thought of ever being interested in dong this. Can you see what I meant about God answering me in his own way? We have to have patience and wait upon God; he always knows what is best for us. Now maybe something I say in this book will help you in some way.

I want to thank my wife Ann for her ideas and help on the remembering part and also my daughter-in-law Sue Everhart for her typing that I could not get anyone else to do. After one year of trying she did it in about two weeks. Thanks a lot girls.

I want to live a long healthy and prosperous life but I have discovered that it is up to me to do some things to have this happen. (God) has promised us seventy plus years(Psalms 90:10) the days of ouryears are threescore years and ten, seventy years or even if by reason of strength fourscore years eighty, yet is there pride (additional years) only labor and sorrow for it is soon gone and we fly away (The Amplified Bible).

Would you like to live to be seventy or eighty or even more if you feel like it and live in a healthy and prosperous life? Psalms 90:10 was for servants (Old Testament Israel).(IIIJohn 1:2) beloved I pray that you may prosper in every way and that your body may keep well even as I know your soul keeps well and prospers. New Testament Sons III John 3:2.

Psalms 23:10 was under the old covenant, if promise was good then how much better it is under the new better one. Which is best old or new when your coat gets old you throw it away for a new better one. (Hebrews Chapter 8&9).

We have to understand our bodies are the home of our spirit (or called heart). This Spirit is from God. We have to teach ourselves to walk and live by this Spirit not by our heads. This Spirit wants to live in our bodies a long time and be Healthy and Prosperous. But it can't if we obey our heads and not our Heart. The attitude of our heart has to be the (God Kind of Love). We are not created to live in our own power (but in the power of love). This love has to be the love that (Jesus) had when he was on earth. This is the (God Kind of Love) not the human love.

How can we have this love? Simply ask (God) to help you practice. Romans 13:10 (Real love works no ill to his neighbor). If you can do this it covers all Ten Commandments. But it takes determination on our part. When you fail Repent and ask God to help you and keep on going. Don't give up nor give in. Feel the difference in your life (feelings-Satisfaction in your walk).

You may have a good life now money, home, car and children, but there is a better life when you walk in the (God Kind of Love). It makes you feel better about yourself. You have to forgive yourself and love yourself before you can love your neighbor with this kind of love. And when problems come up you can say (problem) you can not live in this body because the (God Kind of Love) lives in my heart. (Ezekiel 11:19 Old Testament) God promises to remove stony heart and replace it with a heart of flesh (heart of love) compassion.

We can't have faith in the promises of God until we have the (God Kind of Love) for our neighbor or (enemies or friends). (Galatians 5:6) Faith will not work without real love. Faith will not work for you if you're not walking in the (God Kind of Love).

(Corinthians 13:13) says now abide Faith Hope and Charity these three but the greatest of these is Charity (Love). When you say or do something wrong you are the first one to know you have done so. This is when you want to repent and ask God for help so as not to do that again. Our biggest problem is we tend to talk to quick; we need to think before we talk. When you get the (God Kind of Love) in your heart and not live in your head you will also get compassion and understanding of other people and you will also watch what you say to other people. God's love will help you from hurting other people and give you a better understanding of how to help your brother or sister.

You have got to (want) a better kind of life to correct yourself and put your neighbor before yourself. (Jesus) said love your neighbor as yourself, this is saying a lot this is hard to do. There are five things that work together when you start to practicing (God's) love in your everyday life (Compassion-Forgiving-Understanding-Wisdom and a Sincere Heart) before God. We need to get rid of pride, envy and hate for the enemy will try to use these thing to trip you up and make you fall. You have to understand that the (God Kind of Love) that is in your heart is greater than the enemy that is in the world (I John 5:4). All this takes a lot of work (a self discipline). In other words it takes a strong man or women to live this kind of life but it is so well rewarded and satisfying. It will make you feel good about yourself and others. This (God Kind of Love) will make a new person out of you. You will not believe the change in your every day life.

It will open new doors in your life. The Bible says the old things have passed away behold (all) things are become (new) when you have the (God Kind of Love) in your heart. This (God's) love is already in your heart (in your spirit). This spirit is from (God). Some people say nobody loves me, they don't understand to get love you have to give love (The God Love) and you can't give something you don't have. But if you have this (God) love people can feel it, even animals can feel it in you by just being around where you are. This love is different from the love the world has to offer or (Human Love). We have to understand (any thing that's done without God's Love means nothing).But if you have the (God Kind of Love) you will have the fruits of the spirit working in your life and that's when the better life begins. (Galatians 5:22 thru 26) people will want to be around you because they can feel something different about you. You will never have this to happen to you if you listen to your head.

The (God Love) is the only thing that is going to make your prayers come to pass. If you want to help someone in a problem you have to help yourself first. God looks on the heart not on the flesh. The flesh wants something all the time, no matter good or evil. (Samuel 16:7) But when God looks on heart (spirit) he sees good (he hears every prayer we think) and with God's love we can overcome any problems. Learn not to listen to your head but your heart (spirit).

Gods love is patient and kind not jealous or boastful, it is not arrogant or rude and it does not insist on its own way. It's not selfish or resentful, it does not rejoice at anything wrong. But Gods love will (hold up in anything and bear anything). (I

Corinthians 13) When you get this (Gods Love) in your heart (Spirit) all bitterness, anger and malice will leave you .By this people will know God lives in your heart (John 13:35) and you are a different person. You want to know the secret to receiving Gods best in your life and all the good blessings that he has planed for you? Here it is (Love Your Neighbor as Yourself and Love Your Enemies). If you want to stay healthy and prosperous and live a long life you have to practice trying to help people that did you wrong. Pray for them; let your light shine in on a dark hill. Let your light be a guide to get them to where you are at so you can pass the blessings on to them just like a lighthouse guides ships to safety. By this time if you have read all scripture I have given you, you should know what kind of love I'm talking about.

For physical training is of some value (useful for a little while) but Godliness (spiritual training) is useful and of value in everything and in every way. For it holds promise for the present life and also for the life to come (The Amplified Bible) (I Timothy 4:8). Please read scripture over a couple times and think what it is saying. Practicing this (Gods Love) promises blessings not only in this life but in the life to come. This is proof that walking in the (Godly) exercise only helps in this life but walking in (Gods Love) is going to help in the life to come. So we see walking in (Gods) love not only gives us blessings in this life it will also give us blessings in the next life. We have to do some things for ourselves. We have to put forth a true effort to do our best to live for those blessings that come from (Gods Love) way of life.

Now let's talk a little about faith it goes along with this (Gods Love Way of Life). I have listened to faith messages for 38 years, never but one time have I heard that faith without (Gods Kind of Love) will not work. I've heard faith without works is dead. I guess they both are the same but never knew it until I heard it put this way; Faith Hope and Charity (Love) (Gods Kind of Love) one will not work by its self. Faith without love will not work, hope without love will not work, they all go together. Hope has to come first, you have to have something to hope for to be able to have faith to get it. (Hebrews 11:1 says faith is the substance of things hoped for but the evidence of things not seen. Most folks say oh I have faith but they have never been taught how important that having this (Gods Kind of Love) in their heart (Spirit) is and they wonder why their faith is not working. Sometimes God will let their faith work in little things, it depends on the attitude of their (spirit) at the time. Faith will work all the time if our attitude is right and we ask according to his word. But we are not getting the blessings that God (wants) to give us.

If we are not careful (the enemy) will steal our blessings that (God) wants to give us by (saying); oh the bible says just have faith that's all you have to do and it will come. The bible says he (the devil) is coming and he is for sure. He (the enemy) is just waiting to trick us in such a manner that we just don't see it. Well we have to put ourselves on guard when talking to people, mostly Christians, I have been hurt and I have been done wrong by more Christians then people of the world. There are a lot of (professors) but very few (processor's). I think a lot of these Christians are like this because of the lack of right bible teachings, not all but a lot of them. A lot do not study the bible. If you want to become mature in God and partake of the good things that God wants to give us, you have to study the instruction book he gave us to study every word carefully. Not decide I'm going to read the bible all the way through but you have to ask God to show you what he wants you to know. The Bible says ask and it shall be given to you. This all falls in the line of Faith.

Some say I can not understand what I'm reading. I have been reading for 38 years and I still don't understand a lot I read, that does not matter. If you could understand all that you read your brain would blow out the top of your head.If youunderstand one word that's great. God can take one word and build a conversation on it. Just get in the New Testament and read, start in Corinthians; (God) will do the rest.

The word will revive your spirit and you will understand just what the Bible means, When it says the old things have passed the away behold all things have become new (II Corinthians 5:17).

The enemy does not want you to be knowing what the word is teaching you. He does not come to you in some big manner he comes to you in small things. Here a little there a little to steal your knowledge of this (God Kind of Love) so that your Faith will not work. Think about what this verse (II Corinthians 5:17) is saying; old things are passed away, old ways of thinking, old ways you feel about your enemies, old habits, all things have become new. You still have the old body but a new (want to). A lot of Christians have never felt this, something is wrong with this picture. Is the Bible wrong? I don't think so, pleasure is what you do happiness is who you are. Happiness is only found in the

(Gods Kind of Love). All things become new, the word (all) leaves nothing you can think of out.

This means if we want this happiness and satisfaction that God has for us we have some decisions to make. It's not easy to live this (Kind of Life. But at least we have peace and satisfaction and the blessings to go with it. But living without Gods help is not easy either, Its hard physically and mentally. And no rewards in the next life and not many rewards in this life, none you can depend on. But God will never leave us or forsake us, we are never alone he is with us 24-7. To me this means an awful lot to know that I never have to feel alone. I even have something to say about when I am going to die. (Proverbs 10:27) says the fear of the Lord prolongs your days. (Proverbs 3:1) forget not my law an keep my commandments, for length of days and long life and peace shall they add to you, keep mercy and truth in your life and in your heart and you will find forever and good understanding in yourself and other people. Learn to walk in this (God Kind of Love) and enjoy a happy peaceful life of joy. This (God Kind of Love) in your heart (Spirit) will say to you when you start to say or do something that will hurt somebody (don't do that) and you will say to yourself now where did that come from. That's from the spirit in you.

Some folks have the wrong idea about God. They think he is some big guy up there just waiting for us to do something wrong. But this is not true he is a loving Father who loves his children with an (everlasting) love not a love that turns sour when we do something wrong. It hurts him and makes him sad especially when we don't ask him to forgive us. He goes right on loving the same way and when we ask for forgiveness he throws these things in the sea of forgiveness as far as the east is from the west. He wants to bless us with (everlasting) blessings. He loved us so much that he gave the best thing in heaven (his son) to die on a cruel cross. So if we do something wrong we can be forgiven, if we forgive our neighbor and we can keep right on going and trying to do better and never loose his love for us that is great in my book. We never have to worry about losing our relationship with him. All we have to worry about is keeping this (God Kind of Love) in our heart and work at breaking the curse that has been handed down from generation to generation in our lives. Maybe you say there is no curse in your life, well that's good for you but remember any attitude that is not from God is a curse. The Bible says he that carries not the spirit of God is not of God and there is only two spirits in the world (Good and Evil).

I carried a generation demon in my life from birth until I was 65 years old and never knew it. I served God for 30 of those years the best I knew how and I never played church. I always tried to serve and treat people right but was never taught these things in church. I studied my bible just about every day but was blind to these facts until God opened my eyes.

Now I live in a whole different attitude of my heart. I fought this curse for three or four years before I saw much of a difference but now I am more at peace and more satisfied with my life. I am just sorry that it is so late in life for me to be learning more about this better life. I just thank God that he has opened my eyes; you can know this better life while you are younger and then pass it on to other people while you are enjoying the better life. But you have to accept the Lord in your heart (a one on one) relationship with him, he will take care of the rest. He will change the (want to) in you and by doing this if there is a curse in your life (big or little) you will want to break it and you will see it. Satan will do everything he can to hide it from you, he is very, very smart. But greater is he that is in us than he that is in the world. You might think that I have these subjects all mixed up but I have to write this book as God gives me the words and the subjects. I don't have enough memory left to keep subjects separated. When you get to be seventy years old you don't have much memory left but please bear with me. I have a lot to share with someone if they listen. I promise you it will help you in days to come. The days are coming when you will need some of this stuff to sustain you.

I have learned the hard way that the only way to live, is live in the (God Kind of Love) way. God is the only way. Don't go tochurch or profess God in your life, be a doer of God not just a hearer. The bible says in (John 13:35) by love all men will know we are his disciples not by faith or hope but by our love for one another. This is what makes us Christians, not just going to church and telling people we are Christians. I can put $700. in a suit and $200. in a pair of shoes and walk down the street and tell people I am a rich man but that does not make me rich. But if I take you to the bank and show you ten million in cash that is what makes me rich. It works the same way in a Christian's life. When we show the love one to another we are showing the proof of our being a Christian.

(John 8:31-32) if you continue in my love than you are my disciples indeed. You shall know the truth and the truth will make you free. Free from what? Free from a life of emptiness, a life of no peace, a life of not knowing what to do next, of depression, no satisfaction and a lot more stuff that we have to go through with in this life. The (Lord) said in his prayer to the father that he prayed for his disciples and for us living today. (John 17) that we should not be taken out of this hardship or world, but that the father be with us in spirit, in other words never to leave us 24-7.(Verse 15) this prayer was not just for the disciples but also for us today. (Verse 20) neither pray I for these alone but for them also which shall believe in me through theirs or our word. So you see this is of those decisions we have to make. The important one, please read this chapter (John 17) there is a lot to help you here in that prayer. This is still a part of faith. Remember what I said earlier, faith without (The God Kind of Love) is not working.

Now lets talk about something else that pertains to (Faith) and the (God Kind of Love). Like healing, I have testimony on healing. In 1965 I had never been to a doctor from the time I was a small child. I was driving a 18-wheeler at the time I started to have trouble with my stomach hurting, it kept getting worse and worse. I wouldn't go to the doctor because I had never had any medical problems in my past 15 or 20 years and thought it would pass. But it didn't it just got worse, so bad I could hardly stand it. Everybody talked me into going to the doctor. Well it turned out to be a gastric ulcer in the top of my stomach, plus that's not all one lung was partly collapsed and I had been smoking for years. So I asked the doctor if smoking is what did this to my lung. He said he had patients that never smoked not even one cigarette and had bad lungs. He also said cigarettes were not going to help, the only thing that would help was to quit. So when I left his office I never had another craving for another smoke to this day. I think he scared the craving out of me. Not really, I really think that God was trying to tell me something because I was not saved or going to church at this time. So I quit driving a truck and went to work in a factory. Now about this ulcer, the doctor gave me some nasty pills to take and a diet of no acids like poached eggs and he said I should never eat anything with acid in it. I lived this way for two or three years then I got tired of taking the nasty pills and eating the nasty food. One day I decided to throw away the nasty pills and I started going to church. The preacher was a faith preacher. I started studying the bible day and night. I asked God to heal me or kill me. Well he did neither for a couple of weeks. Some days I thought I was going to die it hurt so bad but finally it quit hurting and I don't know when it quit, it just came to me that it didn't hurt anymore. It has never hurt since. That was in 1967 and I can eat anything I want and it never bothers me. I was trying to serve God to the best of my ability. I still had a lot of bad habits and still have some but God understands this. He died on the cross so he could forgive us when needed. We have to keep putting forth the effort to do what is right , live by our heart not our head. We are going to fail or do wrong, but when we do we will be the first one to know it and God will always be there to pick us up and love us. This is the kinds of love that we have to carry all the time for other people (All the People). This was just one time God has healed me, there are many more times.

Like now I have not been sick not even a cold, nothing for twenty years. I believe that if we can get this (God Kind of Love) in our hearts and live by that love and (do no ill to our neighbors) as the Bible says in (Romans 13:10) we can stay healthy and not be sick. We have to take care of our body because after all our body is not like our spirit it is made of flesh. It is like a car, if its not taken care of it will break down. The Bible says what ever a man sows in life he will reap. If he sows a bad seed, he will reap bad fruit or bad things in life. Sow good things and he will reap good fruit or (blessings in life).If a farmer sows corn he reaps corn, if he sows flowers he reaps flowers, if he sows thorns which are (sticky or bad) (Galatians 6:7&8).I hear preachers all the time say this is not for Christians, I don't believe that. I don't believe Paul was writing to the sinners in Galatians, I believe he was writing to Christians. The reason I believe this is that when I look back over my life I see things I have to do now reflects back to something I did back before I was converted. I to believe God has forgiven us and also he has taken those things and made them acceptable to us now, made them easy to bear. God is a loving and caring Father. He does not want us to be hurting because of our past mistakes. So he makes those mistakes as learning lessons for us as the old saying goes, I know what you mean, I've been there to. I would not want to live my mistakes over but I would not take anything for the learning experience. God does not hold our past against us, but there is a price to pay for every decision we make in this life, we have to live it by our decisions. Good decisions brings good price but bad decisions brings a bad price. This goes for everybody, sinner or saint. For the saint he has someone to go to for help. He will not take the thing away but he will go through it with you. All we have to do is keep a loving attitude in the matter. The good thing is he will never leave us, he is always there wanting to help us.

If we only knew what he has prepared for us in blessings it would blow our mind. I'm talking about in this life. If he could just get us to obey his two commandments (Love God with all our Heart First and Love our Neighbor's as ourselves). This loving everybody with the (God Kind of Love) is a real task. You see God needs us almost as much as we need his blessings. We are the only thing he has to work through to reach the lost sheep. We are to be like a piece of water pipe open at both ends. He speaks to us and blesses us and in turn we are to bless someone else. In one end of the pipe and out the other. God does not come down here like in the (Old Testament) and talk to us. He speaks to us in spirit. If our spirit is in shape to hear (His) voice, or sometimes he speaks to us through another human or anything or anybody that he can get to carry the message, even an animal sometimes. But if through a human make sure that the human's message lines up with the word. There are a lot of false prophets going around giving messages from somewhere else other than God.

When Jesus died on the cross he gave all his power to the (God Kind of Love) Christians before he left. He said greater things you will do than him because he had to go back to the (Father oh the Power that we have). There is a price to pay to be able to use this power. That price all lies in this (God Kind of Love) in our heart (spirit) being used, seen and felt. (He) has no human power on earth now, it is all in the saints if they will do those two commandments (Love your Neighbor as yourself). Love God with all your heart. Soul and mind (Romans 8-9. The bible says he that does not posses the (Spirit of God) does not belong to God. To further prove this (Romans 8-14) for all who are led by the (Spirit of God) are sons of God. In other words we have to walk the walk not just talk the talk. This does not mean we can not have any fun in this life. Jesus said (I come to give you life more abundantly). Does this sound like he doesn't want us to have any fun and laughter and be happy. Does this mean we are not to mingle with sinners or peoples, Jesus ate and drank with sinners or peoples of the world but he did not get involved in their sins? He just sat and told them about the goodness of God (Mark 2:15-17 is Jesus together with his disciples. He sat at the table in his (Levi's) house and many other collectors of taxes and persons (definitely stained) with sin were dining with him for there were so many who walked the same road or (followed with) him, (16) and the scribes (belonging to the party) of the Pharisees, when they saw that he was eating with these definitely known to be especially wicked sinners and the hated tax collectors and said to his disciples; why does he eat and drink with tax collectors and (notorious sinners), and Jesus heard it. He said to them , those who are strong and well have no need of a doctor but those who are weak and sick, I come (not) to call the (righteous) ones torepentance (or conversion)but (sinners) the erring ones and all those not free from sin (Matthew 9:13) So we see this Christian life is not just what a lot of Christians say it is. My wife was told the other day that they could never go into a beer joint, that if the

Lord would come while in there they would go to hell. To hell phooey, this person doesn't know what the word says.

Folks we have to study the Bible to know whether what is said or preached is true or false. This person only knows what some preachers have said. We have to understand (God) is holding us responsible for ourselves. We have to study to know what is right and wrong. There is (no middle of the road) in relationships with God.

God is a merciful God and he goes to great length to reach us so he can give us great blessings that he has for us. He will use anybody or anything to reach us sometimes. This is the kind of love we have to have foreverybody and this is very hard for us to get in this groove. If we put forth the effort seriously (He) will help us, this is not to say that we will not fail at times. But he will always be there to help us. The Bible says in (Corinthians 5:17) old things have passed away we are a new person we still have the same body but the inside has a new person, new blessings, a happier way of life. To have this happier way of life we have to be serious about this. There are some hardships but we just have to keep on trucking. It will always work out if we put these hardships in (Gods) hands and let him work them out.

Now lets go a little deeper in this new life. Let's talk a little about Spirits, this word (spirit) scares some people but spirits will not hurt us. We are a spirit; this body is just a house for us to live in. When God looks at us he looks on our spirit not our body. In the Old Testament days God didn't live in us but from Jesus dying on the cross and going back to God the Father the Holy Spirit lives with our spirit in this body. There are only two spirits in this world, Gods spirit and the devils spirit. This is why (Romans 8:9) now if any man (have not) the spirit of Christ he is none of his. Now think about that for a moment. How many people do you know that goes to church every service, claims to be a Christian and does not have the love and compassion for people that does not go to church and live like them. Is this the attitude that Jesus had when he was on earth? The Bible says Jesus went about doing good (Act 10:38). We as disciples have to walk those same steps after all we are supposed to be ambassadors of Christ and if we don't walk in his footsteps and have the love and compassion that he had for outsiders we are not (under the spout where the honey comes out of) or blessings. Once you get under the spout you don't want to get out. It feels good to be there. We can depend on our spirit to lead us in the right direction at the right time, to do the right thing and to not do things to stop the flow of blessings for us and for our neighbors. Our blessings are to be passed on to our neighbors. God does not give us blessings to keep them all for ourselves. I am not saying we are to give all the blessings to others, I'm saying God always gives enough for us and also enough to give away, share with others what God has shared with us.

The Bible says those who walk by the Spirit will not fulfill the desires of the flesh for the flesh desires against the Spirit and the Spirit against the flesh for these are antagonistic to each other (continually understanding and in conflict with each other). So that you are not free but are prevented from doing what you desire to do (Galatians 5:16-17) (Amplified Bible). So you see this is the two spirits that I just talked about. Some folks think that this evil spirit doesn't bother them but they don't read the bible or they would know better. Some even go to church every service and depend on what the preacher tells them to be right. He may sound right but is still wrong and they will go on believing it instead of getting out their bible and proving it by word. If they did this they would find out a lot of things he says is wrong, not everything but maybe one thing at a time. After all he is just human like us; he is subject to mistakes. Maybe not meaning to, but still does. I know this for a fact I have had this happen to me many times. Matter of fact I still see it happen all the time on TV. This is one way the evil spirit works (a little here a little there) sort of sneaks up on us. The Bible says that little foxes spoil the vine and when the vines are destroyed so is the branches and leaves. (Solomon 2:15 take for us the foxes, the little foxes that spoil the vineyards (of our love). For our vineyards are in blossom young. One day the angels went before the Lord (the devil went to) (Job 1:6) now there was a day when the sons of God (angels) came to present themselves before the Lord and Satan (the adversary and accuser) also came among them. This tells us the enemy is always close by us, this spirit can be seen in different attitudes in people. Did you ever talk to someone and you could feel something good in them, not different but good. The enemy can fool you if you are not careful. He can present himself as an angel of light but that person has an attitude that you don't see very often. The Bible says try the Spirit and see if they are of God. Just mention something about the Lord, mostly the enemy doesn't like that.

Living the (God Kind of Love) life is a one day at a time life. This is what God likes to see in his children. He wants us to depend on him for things we need from day to day. If we can just control our (mouth) and keep the attitude of love, the joy of the Lord will be our strength and we will enjoy a life of health and happiness.

Most important we are preparing for the after life (Eternal) is a long time. We are preparing for a much better life than the (God Kind of Love) life. We have here on earth a place where there is no sickness, no depressed times, no need for wife-husband, money, no hard times. We will be as angels of God. We will be in a spiritual body, no aches no pain of any kind, just spiritual.

Jesus gave his life on the cross so that his life could be in us and his life is in us if we have the (God Kind of Love) in our heart or spirit. When we do this we are living in the stage of eternal life, this is what we receive when we receive Jesus sincerely in our heart. (II Corinthians 5:17-18 Therefore if any be in Christ he is a new creature old things are passed away, behold all things are become new and all things are from God who hath reconciled through Jesus us into himself (received us into favor, brought us into harmony with himself) and gave into us the ministry of reconciliation (that by word and deed we might aim to bring others into harmony with him). Getting back to the water pipe ideain one end out the other, take in and give out, just like we do money.

Despite the things that are going on in your mind right now or the things that you have experienced in your past or the things you think you might be facing in the future. There are miracles just waiting for you like what happened to my wife back in 1976. She started bleeding until the blood ran down her legs. She had been on birth control pills for four or five years. When she went to the doctor he said she had cancer and had to have her womb taken out and could not have any more children. She decided to trust God for healing, she got in the word of God and prayed. She cleaned her six room house while still bleeding and kept on praying until the blood stopped that day. Then on January 1977 she got pregnant and in 1977 she had a healthy boy. That has been 27 years ago and still healed.

The Bible says if you live the (God Kind of Love) life that no plaque shall come near your dwelling. God takes care of his own. (Stay under the spout where the honey comes out). We have to tell ourselves all the time that Jesus lives inside of us 24-7. Nothing can live there except what comes by love (Real Love). We have to live by the decisions we make so take your decisions to God first before making them. God is faithful, he will never forsake you. You have to listen when he says no. We sometimes don't want to hear no but we want to hear yes, so whatever a man sows that man will reap. We don't sow corn to reap grapes. If we sow badly we reap badly, if we sow good we reap good. (Galatians 6:7-8) (Job 4:8) be not deceived God is not mocked for whatsoever a man sows that he also reap. For he that sows to his flesh reap corruption but he that sows to the spirit shall of the spirit reap life everlasting. This is the law of sowing and reaping. We see this as another one of those things we have to do and watch the decisions we make and the seeds we sow. If we can just keep our heart and mouth right and keep asking God to help us to hear his voice (still small voice) when he speaks to our heart (Spirit) and says no and we say yes Lord, everything will be alright. But it is hard to say yes Lord when it is something that we really want or want to say or do. Here is a good example; I went to buy a car. I found one I really liked and took a ride in it. Something was not right I had a funny feeling about this car so I went back to the lot and was talking to the salesman trying to decide. I still had that funny feeling about this car, another person came up to the salesman and wanted the car. The salesman said to me do you want the car or not (that still small voice said no). But I wanted the car so I said yes I will take it (the worst decision I ever made), the car has been nothing but trouble ever since, can't even trust it to go across town. Never, never make quick decisions if God wants you to have that thing or to say that thing, that thing will be there forever. Nothing can take it whatever it is. If God be for us who can be against us (Romans 8:31. The devil is smart, he is right there on your shoulder all the time trying to deceive you, always trying to steal your blessings and he will if we let him. What I should have done was said; I'll be back tomorrow. But I had made the wrong decision and it was too late now I have to live with that decision.

Let's talk a little about Satan the ruler of the world. Satan has no authority over God fearing Christians but he has his influence on us. He is a liar, a thief and a deceiver. At one time he was the high ark angel in heaven. He was a covering cherub in the midst of the stones of fire (Ezekiel 28:13) Let's read, you were once an (ampler of perfection, full of wisdom. perfect in beauty) you were in Eden (not Adams garden) the garden of God. Every precious stone was yours covering Diamond, Crystallite, Jasper. Sapphire, Carbuncle, Emerald, the Gold of which your flutes and tambourines are made of. All were prepared on the day of your creation. You were on the Holy Mountain of God. You were (blameless in your ways from the day of your creation until the (day when evil) was first found in you. Your heart had swollen with pride on account of your beauty. You have corrupted your wisdom for the sake of your splendor, so I cast you out of the Mountain of God.

So we can see here that (Satan was a created Angel in Heaven). He is the next highest power under Jesus the Christ and he was ruler of this earth at one time until he sinned. A lot of people even Christians think he is not real. The Bible says he can make himself an angel of light (II Corinthians 11:14). We have to be careful in our actions and words not to be deceived by him. This is what he wants to do so to rob us of our blessings. If he can do this he will work on us to get us discouraged and we will fall back in the rut again. If we read the Bible and pray every day seriously we will keep the victory and stay under the (spout where the honey flows out) and say to our sickness; out of this body it's the home of the Holy Spirit and Light and Darkness. Dare not mix, keep the light there and there will be no darkness.

There was a time when the angels of God went before God and guess whom went with them, the Devil (Job 1:6. So don't think your going to church or any place else to get away from Satan. He is always around trying to influence us, to do or say something wrong and always when we least expect him to be there. It is hard to keep our minds on the right things to do and say when so many things are going on around us all the time. Always something or somebody is doing something to rile us up and we loose our victory. This is why it is so important for us to read our Bible and pray every day. The best time to do this is in the morning as soon as our feet hit the floor, before we get off the bed. God help me today to do right by my fellow man and at night God forgive me any wrong I did today. God is faithful and merciful, he will help you and we have to teach ourselves to pray always through the day. This takes time to get this (God Kind of Love) in our hearts but this is the way it is done. God will help us do all things. Jesus said if you love me keep my commandments only two; (love God with all your being and your neighbor as yourself). If we do these two commandments everything else will fall in place. Its hard to do but so is the world hard to live in without God in your life. But oh the reward we get by living this (God Kind of Love). Now the Devil will do everything he can to try to distract you, because he knows the result is going to hurt his work. He likes to control our mind (spirit) this is where that (God Kind of Love) in our heart comes in. He can't control anything that is in Gods hands. We have the power (authority) to resist his control over our minds (St Luke 10:19).

Our Father is a loving God who will not allow us to be tempted more than we can bare (I Corinthians 10:13) We have been chosen through Jesus (before) the foundation of the world (Ephesians 1:3-4) now the world is billions of years old and with God Saint Peter says one day is as a thousand years. So we are chosen a long time ago. We have been predestined. Let's read Gods work in peoples lives delivered from sin. (John 12:26) if anyone serves me he must follow me (too Cleve steadfastly to me) conform wholly to my example in living and if need be dying and wherever I am there will my servant be also and if anyone serves me my Father will honor him. (Romans 8:28-29-30-31) for we know that all things work together for the good to them that love God. To them that are called according to his purpose for those he did fare knew (of whom he was aware and loved beforehand). He also destined from the beginning foreordaining them to be molded into the image of his son and share inwardly his likeness that he might become the first born among many Brethren those whom he thus fare ordained he also called and those he called also justified (acquitted) made righteous putting into right standingwith himself. Those whom he justified he also glorified, raising them to a heavenly dignity and condition or stage of being. So if God be for us who can be against us. Man! What a mouthful, there is so much to cover in this book its hard to get it out of my mind and on paper. The Devil is fighting me all the time. The Devil is trying to confuse me but he is a liar. I will finish this book if it takes me the rest of my life. So we were predestined before the world was formed. God knows where we live and will visit us one way or another.

The Devil is mad and working in this world but so are the Father and his son Jesus. The Devil is walking to and fro in this world seeking whom he can get. Discouraged and down and out he knows when we are this way he has more of a chance to talk to us and get us off track and back in that same old rut.

Let's talk a little about this rut. A rut is a place you get into and can't seem to get out ofand if by any chance you find a place where you can steer yourself out of the rut then we try to stay out of that rut the next time. Although there are times we get in one and cannot get out of this rut without help. If you are reading this book that tells me you want some answers about this life. I don't know what your problems are but I do know the answer to them is to get a one on one relationship with Jesus, not a relationship with your friends. When you put Jesus first not second in your heart, not mother, father, sister, brother, children or mate but first, your problems will be his problem and they will seem like nothing to you then. You will have a partner to fight those problems in the future with you. Remember God will never let you be tempted more than you can bear. (I Corinthians 10:13) there is no temptation taken you but such as is common to man. But God is faithful who will not suffer you to be tempted above what you are able, but with that temptation also make a way to escape that you may be able to bear it all and we must remember that all things happen to the good to those who love the Lord and are called according to his purpose. (Romans 8:28) God has a purpose for everyone. We all have a destiny to fulfill. God has made the way, it is up to us to choose that way and to find that way is in his word. He has given us free choice it is up to us to choose the way of peace and happiness. We have to be doers of the word not just hearers of the word. We have to talk the talk but we have also to walk the walk. It is easy to talk the talk but we can't walk the walk without the (Love of God) in our heart (spirit). The Bible says if any man hath not the Spirit of Christ he is none of his. A lot of Christians carry a good spirit in church but when they get out of church they carry another spirit. For about three years I would not go to any church because I knew something was wrong with the picture until I read that Jesus said; plant seed of wheat and when it grows up, weeds grow up together with the wheat and when harvest comes that's when the wheat and weeds will be separated. So we have to bite the bullet and keep on.

Right Teaching

Again I think a lot of Christians are this way because of lack of right teaching, I know when I was coming up in this Christian life I can never remember of one sermon taught on the (God Kind of Love) and sometimes you can read and read and never see what you are reading. I have read about this (God Kind of Love) in the bible for years and never knew what I was reading until someone else opened my eyes to it. Although I knew there was something wrong in the churches and in most Christians lives for most of my Christian life and in my own life until God opened my eyes a couple of years ago and I started to study on it and started to find some things in my life like a Generation Demon. Don't laugh there is a lot of Generation Demons around, they are mostly mean Demons handed down from Generation to Generation.

Have you ever heard the old saying "Like father Like Son"? Well when father died that Demon jumped from father to son or daughter. The one I carried was handed down from grandfather to mother to son. This Demon can be broken at any Generation if that Generation knows it and wants to break it. But it can only be broken through Jesus Christ and it has to be broken with this (God Kind of Love) in the heart.

Jesus told his disciples preach the gospel and start at home. The (God Kind of Love) is the Gospel. But first we have to preach it to ourselves and accept Jesus as our Savior and also our Lord. I call him "THE BOSS" because the Boss is the Boss right or wrong he is still the Boss. But this Boss will never be wrong. A lot of times it sure looks like he is wrong, but if you just wait a while it will all turn out right.

These Christians who are untaught about the (God Kind of Love) mostly have been taught to just accept Jesus and everything else will be alright, not so, we have to accept Jesus alright but we have to accept him not only as our savior but as lord of our life too.

Now we have to stop and think what Lord of our life means. It is like if you buy a machine and you get a book of instructions of how you put it together it will not go together any other way. You may be able to make it work by putting it together your way but it will not be right. This same material thing also applies in the Spiritual. God gave us an instructional book to go by to put our life together. We have to go by the book you might say well I can't do that you are right. You can't by yourself (but) when you make Jesus and Lord he will (always) be there to your Savior help you.

This is where being (Lord of Your Life) comes in, he will not do it (for you but he will go through it with you). You know when you choose Jesus as Savior and Lord you have come into a State Of Kingship. From the time you accept him fully you have the State Of Kingship in your life and it is up to you to walk the walk as well as talk the talk. This will not happen over night it has taken quite a while to get in the rut and it will take a while to get out and learn how to stay out of the rut. Jesus will never leave you he will always be there to help you. Now sometimes he wants to take you to a higher level and he will stand back and let you work things out yourself but he is right there guiding you and you will not know it until later.

The bible says we are made a little lower than God. (Romans 5:17) says for if by one mans offences reigned by one; much more they will receive Abundance of Grace and of the Gift of Righteousness Shell Reign in Life by one Jesus Christ.

(Palms 8:4-5) what is man that than art mindful of him? And son of man that thou united him? For thou hast made him a little lower than angels and has crowned him with Glory and Honor. He has promised us to be Heads not Tails.

(Genesis 1:27) so God created man in his own image in the image of God created he him male and female created he them.

Notice he spoke this two times straight in a row. I believe he made us as close as possible to himself in looks, character, and size and in every way you can think of. Look at Adam he was so smart he named every animal-every fruit-vegetable-fish.

Boy that's smart just think what we would be like now if Adam hadn't given up the leadership of the family and listened to Eve and ate that fruit. Man was made with the life of God within himself. God took his own Spirit and put it within his first creation (man). God loved his creation so much that after 6000 years of living the way Adam chose for us to live he came back to Earth and lived as a human being so that he could make a way for us to get back into a Spiritual State if we chose too. By taking on the Sins of the World and being crucified on a cruel cross the worse kind of death. Every kind of problem we go through today he went through first. Jesus said greater love has man than he lay down his life for his brother.

The average person has never gathered the reality of what Jesus dying on the cross is all about. It is all about his Love for us his kids. (We Are Kings Kids). Now we have to act and do like Kings Kids. And by loving God and our brother the same we can say we are the Kings Kids and he be for us who can be against us. God wants to bless us to the fullest so we can bless others. This is the way God intended it to be in the beginning. In the beginning Adam was the ruler of the world and he gave it over to Lucifer (Satan).

Most people think that when they give their life over to Jesus and get forgiveness that that's all there is to the relationship but that's wrong. We have become ONE Spirit with God. God's Spirit and ours is (one). We are ten times Bigger Inside than on the Outside. We are like Adam was in the garden of Eden By Faith.

(John 14:15-16) if you love me keep my commandments and I will pray the father and he shall give you another comforter that he may abide with you forever The Holy Spirit.

(Corinthians 6:19-20) What? Know ye not that your body is the temple of the Holy Ghost which is in you with your love of God and you are not your own. For you are bought with a price (Christ dying on the cross for us). Therefore Glorify God in your body and in your Spirit which are Gods.

Here we see that the Spirit of God lives in us. When we have this personal relationship with him. In other words God himself lives within us. Think about this a little, this is pretty strong stuff. A lot of people don't believe this but I just gave you Bible that says he does live in us.

Back in the Old Testament days there was a place called the Holy of Holy in the tabernacle it was behind a curtain that weighed 2000 lbs. If anyone tried to go in there but the priest he was struck dead at the door, and the priest could only go there once a year and he had to be purified before going in and he had to wear a gown with bells on the bottom.

(Exodus 28:4) And there are the Garments which they shall make, a Breastplate, a Ephod rope, a broidered corset, a miter and a girdle and they shall make Holy garments for Aaron thy brother and his sons. That he may minister unto me in the priest's office. 28:35 and it shall be upon Aaron to minister and his sound (the bells on the bottom of his garment) shall be heard when he goes in unto the Holy place before the Lord and when he cometh out that he die not.

Folk's things are a lot different now than they were then. God does not live in churches now. Now he lives in us. So you see we have to be careful and take care of this body because its Gods house.

The Bible says it's not what goes in a mans mouth that defines the man but what comes out of the mouth that defines the man.

Matthew 15:18 But these things which comes out of the mouth comes from the heart and the defile the man. So be careful what comes out of your mouth. They will hinder your prayers and your relationship with God, cause your blessings to cease the (honey will stop coming out of the spout). Too many people try to live by traditions and this is stopping the blessings of God. Some say well I'm being blessed and that is true but they are not being blessed the way God wants to bless us. The Bible says Eye has not seen or Ear has not heard what God has (planed for us). If we want what he has planed for us we are going to have to make some decisions to read and study the Bible and start doing what it says and believe what it says.

God is always wanting to take us to a higher level but so many people are satisfied where they are at and if you're satisfied there that's okay for awhile and then it wears off. What they don't understand there is no (stopping place), in this life you are either going up or down and if we are not careful we will wind up back where we started, in that rut and wonder how we got there.

I think if we look back we will find we never had the (Real Love of God) in our hearts .This Love will never fail it will never leave us (This Kind of Love) is what kept Gods disciples going on when (bad times come, and they will come).

A disciple always knows that the Lord is right there with him even though he cannot feel him. He knows he can't walk by feelings. Feelings will deceive you. (You have to know that you know) that he will never leave you or forsake you.

God will never take you on a journey and drop you in the middle. If we keep his Love in our heart we have to watch right from the beginning and make sure there is no other Gods such as money, cars, homes, kids, spouse, party, before him. (He will not take second place in our lives). He refuses to accept anything or anybody before himself. He has to be number one in your life. I have seen churches go on and on for years and years and be blessed to a certain extent and never do much of anything for (God or people). People dying and going to hell and they never will reach out to them because they are afraid they will lose some of their regular fifty people. You walk into these churches and its deader than 4 o'clock. You feel uncomfortable, feel no spirit at all or you feel a spirit that doesn't belong there. You don't feel Gods spirit because nobody brought God there. There is no God in that building, the only God in there is what the people brought there. Because (God doesn't live in Tabernacles he lives in us).

The bible says (traditions has made the word of God of none effect). (Mark 7:13) (Making the word of God of none effect through your traditions which you have delivered and many such things of this kind you are doing)

People have the idea that because they see a preacher preach under a anointing or pray for someone and they get healed or he jumps and hollers and speaks in tongues that this man is a great man of God. Well I don't read in the life of Jesus where he ever jumped and hollered when he taught. When I see this I want to know more about this preacher. I want to know about his home life. (The devil has a anointing too). The Bible says to (try the spirit to see if it is from God). All spiritual action is not from God, some is from the Devil and if you are a disciple of Jesus you will not know the difference unless you have a (Gift of Discerning of Spirits). A lot of people have this gift and as far as praying for someone and they get healed God will use anybody or anything to get what he wants done this is up to God not man. He even used a donkey one time to talk to a man.

(You don't believe all you see in churches); a lot of things that go on there is phony and as far as someone speaking in tongues so does the Devil. Better than any of us the Devil is a deceiver and he will deceive you (any way) he can and he will do it through your Christian friend quicker then through a person not saved. Don't ever think anyone is any better than you just because they have been saved longer than you, because they may be (saved but not converted). Being Saved will not take you no where, to be a disciple of Jesus we have to be Converted not saved. (Act 15:3) And being brought on that way to the church they passed through Phoenicia and Samaria declaring the conversion of the Gentiles and they caused great joy unto all Brethren.

Folks just remember we have to work out our own Salvation with fear and trembling.

(Philippians 2:12-13) Where for my beloved as ye have always obeyed, not as in my presence obey but now much more.

Work out your own salvation with fear and trembling. (2:13) for it is God which work's in you both to Will and to do of his good pleasure. (Romans 8:38-39) The apostle Paul said I am per swayed that nothing (this means anything in life) will separate me from the Love of God. This is the love that I am talking about (The Real Love). If we don't have this love in our heart we don't have conversion. Conversion means born again. (Corinthians 5:17) Says therefore If any man be in Christ he is a new creature, old things are passed away. Behold (all) thingsare become new.

The nice thing about being born again is you can look at people and not have respect of another. The Bible says you shall know them by their fruit. What fruit?

(Galatians 5:22) But the fruit of the Spirit is Love-Joy-peace-Long suffering Gentleness-Goodness-Faith-Meekness-Temperance against such there is no law. (5:24) And they that are Christ's have crucified the flesh with the affection and lusts.

There is a price to pay for everything we do or say in this life. Galatians 6:7 Be not deceived God is not mocked for what so even a man sows (material or spiritual) that shall he also reap.(good or bad) We have to look into a mirror sometimes and say to that man looking back at me and ask him a couple of questions. Who did you do wrong yesterday or hurt by our mouth or lie to.

Folks when things are starting to go wrong in your life better check your Spirit and see where it is coming from, it could be a sign you are doing something wrong. The Great Kenneth HagenSaid one time he had never been sick from the time he was healed from a death. But at the age of sixteen yrs old to the time he died an old man. But there was times he would start getting signs of sickness then he knew something was wrong. He would Repent and ask God to get him back on the Real Love of God track and all signs would leave him.

We have to walk in the lights that God gives us to walk in. We can not walk in some body else's light. (John 1:7)

If we walk in the light as he is in the light we have fellowship (partnership) one with another and the blood of Jesus Christ his son cleanses us from all sins. So many people (Christians) see a preacher performing his ministry that God gave him and they say oh I would like to do that and start trying to walk insame ministry (light) and this will not work. We have to pray and carry this God Kind of Love and let God give us our own ministry. We can't operate in another ministry. God has a ministry for every child of his. It may be sweeping the church floor or cleaning the bathrooms. Do it with all your heart and he might give you a bigger one and take you to a higher level.

God did not make two people alike not even twins. There is some difference there. He might give you the gift ofhelps, to me its one of the most important Gifts of all. You might say how will I know what my ministry is. A lot of times God will put something on your Heart or Spirit to do. Something that you don't believe in or don't want to do. It you can't get rid of the thought it just keeps bugging you. You had better go to the Bible and pray about it ask God to confirm it by the word or someone that you know is a servant of God with fruits in their life or carries the Love of God in their heart (Spirit). Just don't go to any Christian . Most Christians (profess) but don't (posses). They might tell you the wrong thing. It's better to let God show you or confirm it by the Bible. This way you will stay in God's Love and keep your Blessings flowing. Staying under the Spout where the honey comes out.

We have to walk in the footsteps of Jesus and the twelve disciples to keep the Blessings coming and taking no mans word for it without proving it by the Bible. We can not walk by feelings or sight because they will deceive you and you might not even know it till it's too late.

I write the things in this book so you might not fall into some of the traps I have fell in. Once in those traps its hard to get out. I listened and watched other Christians for thirty years being hardheaded before I learned to listen only to God. I'm not putting down all Christians there are about 20% I believe that are God fearing and God loving Christians. The Devil is a smart Character and he will take advantage of every opportunity to deceive you. He will (play with your mind) to try to get you to the point where (he has influence over you) in your mind. (He has no authority over you but he can have influence) over you (if you let him).

Just remember if you carry the Real Love of God in your heart (Spirit) the Devil cannot stay where the Lord is. So this is what you have to tell the Devil-God lives in this body Devil you are a liar and you can't live in this body. Read (Colossians 1:13) Giving thanks to the Father which has made us meet to be partakers of the inheritance of the Spirit in Light. Also 1:13 who has delivered from the power of Darkness (Devil) and has translated us into the Kingdom of his Dear Son. Also read (Ephesians 3:16) That he would grant you according to the riches of his Glory to be strengthened with might by the Spirit in the holy man.

Folks its hard at times to be a disciple of God. It was hard for Jesus at times too. I have lived both lives Sinner and Christian. But I found out that it is so much more rewarding to live the Christian life because there is no reward in a sinner's life but heartache. (Romans 8:16) The Spirit itself barestwitness with our Spirit that we are the children of God and if children then heirs of God and joint heirs with Jesus Christ if so be that suffer with him that we may be also glorified together. Just remember we suffer (in him not for him).

If you accept this Real Kind of Love in your heart and take on conversion in your life be prepared to hear from the Devil. But remember all the past has been forgiven and cast into the sea of forgetfulness. Don't let him try to tell you there is something in your past, anything that was not taken away by God. All there is a lot of things you will remember but that's all. Just remember all things are past away. I gave you the word earlier that proves this. The Devil will always try to use something hanging over your head against you. Don't let him tell you that you have something hanging over your head, you don't. Jesus said in (John 10:28-29) Once you have received Jesus as Lord and Savior no man can pluck you out of his hand and I give them eternal life and they shall never perish. Neither shall any man pluck them out of his hand. (27) My sheep hear my voice and I know them and they follow me. (29) My father which gave them me and he is greater than all and no man is able to pluck them out of my fathers hand.

(Forgiveness,) lets talk a little about forgiveness. If we want to continue in the Blessings we have to know about forgiving. To come to the Lord we have to repent (or turn and go the other way) and ask for the Lord to forgive us or we are not forgiven. It's the same way with people, if we do someone wrong we have to (ask them for forgiveness) or we will (not get forgiveness). That person can forgive you from their heart and you will not get that forgiveness unless you ask for it. This is something that a lot of Christians will not do. Pride will not let them. The Bible says pride goes before a fall Counterfeit Christians can be Religious and be lost. They (know about God but don't know God). (Proverbs 16:18) Pride goes before destruction and a naughty or arrogant Spirit before a fall. (Obadiah 1:3) the pride of your heart hath deceived thee.

A prideful Spirit is a Demon from Hell. The Lord said if you don't forgive, you will not be forgiven by the Lord. (Luke 6:37) Judge not and ye shall not be judged. Condemn not and ye shall not be condemned. Forgive and you shall be forgiven.

Forgiving is something that is hard to do sometimes. Sometimes you have to forgive (even when it is not your fault). But if you feel you should do it you had better do it and bite the bullet. God will (bless you for being obedient). Because if it has stuck with you for a while it probably was God speaking to you. We can't always go by our feelings even though they might be warm and fuzzy. Most of the time when God is speaking it is some thing that we do not want to do and we have the tendency to tell ourselves no that is not God talking to me. But when the thought sticks to you and you can't get rid of it, it is probably

God speaking. Although the Bible says try the Spirit to see and make sure it is God. (John 4:1) Beloved believe not every Spirit but try the Spirits whether they are of God because many false prophets are out in the world. Sometimes we may have to ask a false prophet for forgiveness even though we know they are false. This is when our Real Love of God is tried. When you can do this you can say I believe the Real Love is working. When you can see the Real Love working in your own life then your starting to get into this Blessed Life.

Now we need to talk a little about the next step which is (worshiping the Lord.) Now when I say Worship the Lord I'm not talking about having a preacher preach you into a excitement mode, or goose pimples, or whooping and hollering jumping up and down or speaking in tongues that you can't understand. That's not real worship. Real worship is when you get your mind on God only and praising and thanking God for all the good things he has done for you. If nothing else that you are still breathing. You will get into a place in the Spirit where all your problems and troubles are gone. You are in a place where you will realize that you are not alone. You will know that you know that you will know that you are not alone and all you can do is just cry and cry and cry and all you want to do is worship him. That's when God wants to pull you out of all those old experiences and put a new life in you. If you have come this far you can look back and see some new Blessings already. But God wants to Bless you much much more than you could even think about. And at this point you will want to get rid of some stuff in your life. Just ask God to remove the desire for them and to give you something good to put in their place.

You see it's like a board on a wall being held up by a screw This board has to stay on the wall, its essential that it stays there. If you take the screw out because its rusty you have to put a nail or another screw in it to hold it up. It's the same thing with you when God takes something out of you. Let him put something good back in its place. Here is some scriptures to back up what I just said. (Luke 11:24-25-26) When an unclean Spirit is gone out of a man he walks through dry places seeking rest and finding none. He says I will return to my house where I come out. (25) And when he comes he finds it swept and garnished (clean) (empty). (26) then goes he in and takes(with him seven other Spirits more wicked than himself and enter into the man and the state of that man is worse than he was in the beginning).

So be sure that when something bad goes out something good goes in. In other words when and if God takes some bad Spirits out of you. You feel different your old want to has turned into a new want to. The new want to should be Good Spirits. Remember what I said try the new Spirits to make sure they are of God. Because Satan is a deceiver, he is always walking up and down in the earth looking for someone to devour. (Peter 5:8) Be sober, be vigilant because your adversary the Devil as a roaring lion walks about seeking who he may devour.

By this time you might be saying I could do all these things you are telling me to do. Well sure you can because you by now have a helper within you. All the stuff will come natural. The hard thing to do is to keep your mind on Jesus and listen for the Spirit to speak to your Heart (your Spirit). Because (Satan can transform himself into an Angel of Light). (II Corinthians 11:14) So don't be surprised at some of his tricks he will pull on you he is a sharp cookie. But Greater is he that is in you then he that is in the world. At this point there is something we need to do and that is to pray and ask God to give us a Good Real Christian Friend to have Fellowship with and a second Friend on call 24-7 for help. Read (Ecclesiastes 4:12) and if one prevail against him two shall withstand him and a threefold cord is not quickly broken.

Now you see the word of God has all the tools to work with in this God Kind of Life. It is not as hard as it seems to be. God's Kind of Life sure has a lot of rewards to offer plus eternal life.

One of the things that helped me most of all was get into a good Bible study with some Good Christians. You get a lot of ideas on subjects and also mostly you will find people in Bible Studies are from all walks of life and mostly everyone has found something Spiritual or looking for a better way of life. When you get six or eight people talking about the Bible you find out things that you would not find out so quickly by yourself. But then again don't believe everything you hear and see until you have proven it to be so. Another thing is to find a good Bible (teaching) not preaching church to attend where you feel comfortable and everybody is friendly. This might be hard to find sometimes. We need messages that teach us about everyday life we have to live an not someone to preach us into a wild frenzy experience. We can watch a movie on TV and get that. We need something that will help us live right today and tomorrow. We have worked at this thing too long to loose this Blessed Life over a feeling that will only last a few hours. I have had this happen to me so many times and it's just not worth it. I just get up and walk out when I hear this preacher start to preaching this kind of stuff and that's all it is (is stuff) does not help anybody. There are supposed to be (edifying the body of Christ) (us). Read (Corinth 12:19) Again think you that we excuse ourselves into you? We speak before God in Christ but we do all things Dearly Beloved, for your edifying. Here Paul is speaking about him teaching the brother, the Gospel not for himself but for their help. Also read (Corinth 14:26) & (Corinth 14:12) Paul is teaching us that whatever we say-say to the people for Edification. If what you have does not edify you, don't listen. You can talk to a person ten minutes and tell if he is speaking things to edify you. There is a lot in the Bible about Edifying. So this means it's very important to know about. And if we don't know about something that's important that the Bible speaks about so many times we could be Deceived very easy to the point that we could loose our Blessings and this we don't want to do. So learn all about being edified by your friends. Be careful don't let anything separate you from the God Kind of Love. Even some Christians will talk to you and use words to cut the heart right out of you just like some Sinners will do. The only difference in the two is one (professes) and the (other does not profess) and (neither one possess) God's Love. So we will have to be careful of what we listen or see. We have to go by what God's Word says; it will not lie to us.

Well let's change the subject a little. Let us talk about (Temptation.) Temptation is something that will be with us 24-7 the rest of our lives. It has been with us all our lives so far. And its not going to leave us now. It's just another one of the Devils tools to get the control of our minds. But God has made us a promise to handle this tool of the Devil's. In (Corinthians 10:13)There is (no temptation) taken you but such as is (common to man). But God is Faithful who will not suffer (let) you to be tempted above that you are able, but will with the temptation also make a way to escape that you be able to bear it. (II Peter 2:9) The Lord knows how to deliver the Godly Act of Temptation and to reserve the unjust into the day of Judgment to be punished. You see every time the Devil raises his head in a Godly persons life he gets kicked in his head by God for us. But that does not stop him he will be back. But as I said before greater is he that is in us than he that is in him(or the world). There are many things in the world to temp us, things that we would not think of. The Devil is like a fisherman fishing in the river if he gets no bites here he moves up river or down river he keeps moving until he gets a bite. He is the same with us and he has a lot of playing ground to work with.

There is a little chain you can get to hang around your neck it has a sign on it that reads, What Would Jesus Do. We all should have one of these and keep one hand on it all the time. One other way (strangely) the Devil has is to get you (away from Good Fellowship) to be able (to get to your mind). We know to fight Temptation 24-7 we always have from a baby on up. Think about it awhile how you had to fight Temptation when you were young or when you were out running around in the world and we will always have to. But God will be with us through it all if we are Faithful servants, We have to look at Temptation like this, each time we get the victory over Temptation we are a little stronger in God. There are times when we don't get the victory but if we get right back up and ask God to forgive us he will and keep on going. We have learnt something so you see we have grown a little because God went through it with us. (Matt 6:13) says and don't let us yield to Temptation but deliver us from the evil one. Some people say they are never tempted I don't believe this. But if they are not tempted that means the Devil is leading them and they are Deceived.

Temptation always gets us at our weakest time and our weakest point. What is our weakest point? That's where we have to guard.

You might hear some say I have Willpower enough not to let Temptation get to me. But all Willpower got broken in the Garden of Eden by Adam and Eve. Some also might say they have Self Discipline enough to not yield to be tempted. But you can't overcome sin by Self Discipline. Sin has to be overcome by the (Blood of Jesus or God's Kind of Love). This is what the cross of Christ and his dying was for, so that we could be in Right Standing with God. (Rightness with God) (1 John 1:9) The Living Bible. But if we confess our sins to him he can be depended on to forgive us and cleanse us from every wrong. Just remember all things work together for good to them that Love God to them who are called according to his purpose (Roman 8:28.

Now lets talk a little about this Righteousness Right Standing with God (1 John 1:7)But if we walk in the light as he is in the light we have fellowship or partnership one with another and the Blood of Jesus Christ his son cleanses us from all Sin.

But verse 8 says (if we say we have no Sin we deceive ourselves) and the truth is not in us. Verse 9 if we confess our Sins he is faithful and just to forgive us our Sins and to cleanse us from all Unrighteousness. So if we are cleansed from Sin, that makes us Righteous.

If we keep this God Kind of Love in our hearts and get serious about our Relationship with God the Fruits of the Spirit will work in our lives. We will stay (Under the Spout where the Honey comes out) because we have been given the Gift of Righteousness.

(Hosea 4:6) Says my people are destroyed for lack of knowledge. There arefive things we have to know-Who we are-who God is-our right-our privilege-our dominion and we will never be destroyed by the Devil or loose our Blessings. (Roman 5:17) says we shall Reign (to hold and exercise sovereign power) in life by one Jesus Christ.

This tells us who we are Kings and Priests (Revelation 1:16) and he made us Kings and Priests to God and his Father. You see Jesus was a King, well we are joint heirs with Jesus so we are Kings to. When Jesus went back to be with the Father in Heaven he gave all his powers to us. He said greater things you will do than he done because he has to leave the Earth. But there is some things we have to do to qualify, I have spoke of the things earlier in this book. God made us a free moral agent we can do what we want to, or trust God and make him to beour Savior and become that new person and become Kings and Priests and we know who we are and by knowing who we are we will know who God is. His our Advocate or Lawyer who sits on the Right Hand of God at all times pleads our case to the Father for us. We have the (authority) to go into the Throne Room at any time and talk to Jesus about anything. And don't think that he does not hear you because he hears Every Prayer you "think".

I know because he told me so. We also (have the authority) to do anything that he did when he was on Earth. He has given it to us. This is our right and our privileges and our Dominion. When we realize we have the five things, we will do great things for God and when we give to God (he will give us back a hundred fold in return). (Matthew 6:33) Seek the Kingdom of God and his Righteousness (first) and all the things will be added. I have said before God wants (first place) in our lives and God lives in them who obey his voice.

I have asked God for things and I didn't get them, and later down the road I was glad I didn't get them. Because they would have been a real bad heartache for me. So you have to be careful what you ask God for because you might get it and regret it later on. Be sure you want it. A lot of times we ask God for things and never stop to think about asking God if it is the right thing or if it will Edify someone else or just Edify ourselves or just something we don't need. We need to (think about someone else just as much as we think about ourselves). If we would train ourselves to do this we would (see more Blessings in our lives). (1 John 4:8) He that loves not (his brother) knows not God for God is Love. This ties in with Right Standing with God. The God Kind of Love in our hearts and Loving our Brothers or Sisters (or others).

This is the most important thing in our Christian Life. This is not to say we will never have problems or troubles in our lives. We are going to have them no matter what kind of life we live. God will not take them away from our lives but he has (promised to go through them) with us and help us as we go through them. These problems are going to be around as long as we live. But God will never leave us or forsake us and through every trial we will come out stronger. Its not the trial that we go through but (it's the attitude we carry while going through it). This whole Blessed Life that I'm talking about all hinges on Loving our Neighbors as ourselves and the Attitude we carry all the time. We have to show that we have something in our lives that others don't have. Something so good that they want to know what it is and when we are asked what it is we have to have the right answer for them. This is still the right Standing with God (Righteous) as (The God Kind of Love in our Hearts). We have to pray-study-read to have these answers.

I think the best place to start reading is in the New Testament. The book of Mark then to the book of Acts then on to Romans and on to some of the short books written by the Apostle Paul. The books of 1-2-3 John are the Love Books don't fail to read them. (II Timothy 2:15) Study to show thyself approved into God a workman that needs not to be ashamed rightly dividing the word of truth. I think the thing that professing Christians need now days is to study the Bible more and pray more for God to give them a renewing of their minds, This is the way to get your mind renewed is through study and prayer. (Romans 12:2) And be not conformed to this world but be you transformed by the renewing of your mind that you may prove what is that good and acceptable and perfect will of God. We have to remember that our body and our Spirit are two different things. God will help our Spirit but we have to do something with our body. God will not do anything with our body, he only deals with our Spirit (or heart). God has to deal with our Spirit even after it is converted because our Spirit is not perfect after conversion.

Peter said in (I Peter 2:2) As new born babies desire the sincere milk or (simple things of the word) that we may grow there by so you see we have to make the decision to pray and study so we can grow into maturity. You see we are (or our mind is) responsible for our body. (I Corinthians 9:27) Like a athlete I punish my body treating it roughly training it to do what it should, not what it wants to. Otherwise I fear that after enlisting others for the race I myself might be declared unfit and ordered to stand aside (The Living Bible). If we keep the love of God in our heart or (God Kind of Love) in our heart this Love will help us to control our body to keep doing good and treating our neighbor as our self.

So you see it is real important to keep our minds renewed by the word. By doing this we Stay Under The Spout From Where The Honey Flows Out and our Blessings continue on. If we want to continue being blessed we have to decide to do these things. If we don't the body will take over the mind and we will go back to that old rut again. This is what we don't want; this world is getting harder and harder every day to live in.

Folks we need all the help we can get. It's getting to the point that we are not going to be able to get by in our daily living without a higher power. And with this (God Kind of Love) in our hearts and treating our neighbor as our self we have this higher power. But it's a daily process; we have to take it (Day by Day). Sooner or later this is what it is coming to. We have to understand that this life is not (One Big Party) as a sinner or as a servant of God. But as a servant of God we have someone to go to that we know will never leave us or forsake us. Where else can you find someone you can depend on? We are made just like God looks and all, his (image). What does image mean? God is not going to forsake his own children that he made just like himself or he would not be God. Only the enemy would do that (Satan). (Genesis 1:27) So God created man in his own image in the image of God he him male and female created he them. (II Peter 1:3) According as his divine power has given to us (all) things that (pertain unto life) and (goodness) through the knowledge of him that has called us to his own Glory and his own Goodness. Now read that in the living Bible. (II Peter 1:3) for as you know him better he will give you through his great power everything you need for living a truly Good Life. He even shares his own Glory and his own Goodness and by that, some mighty power he has given us all the other (Rich) and (Wonderful Blessings) he promised. For instance the promise to save us from the lust and rottenness all around us and to give us his (own character). This is what it takes in our life today. The time is coming and from what things look like around the world it won't be very long before the only thing we will have to hang onto is (GOD). I know this is not what a lot of people are saying, but just turn your TV on to a 24/7 news channel and listen to what's going on in the world for about 30 days and you will see what I mean.

Right now I am writing this part of this book three days after the hurricane Katrina came through the Gulf. Things are so bad the Gulf States I can hardly watch it without crying. Put yourself in those folk's shoes. But I noticed those folks that spoke of God in their lives are still going on and still happy.

Folks the things I am putting in this book are not hearsay but my own experience. I have been through a lot in 38 yrs and still have a lot to go through. But I know God will be there right with me. So if God be with you what or who can be against you. So folks you had better get your life together because things are not going to get any better but worse. You had better prepare yourself.

(Let's talk a little about times to come) (I Timothy 4:1-5) The Living Bible The Holy Spirit tells us clearly that in the last time some in the church will turn away from Christ and become eager followers of teachers with Devil inspired idles. The teachers will tell lies with straight faces and do it so often that they're conscience won't even bother them. V3 they will say it is wrong to be married and wrong to eat meat. Even though God gave these things to well-taught Christians to enjoy and be thankful for. V4 For everything God made is good and we may eat gladly if we are thankful for it. V5 and if we ask God to Bless it for it is made good by the Word of God and Prayer. Their verses we should study real close and match them up with today's life, now here is another that is more like today's living. (II Timothy 3:1-5) You may as well know this too. That in the last days it is going to be very difficult to be a Christian V-2 For people will love only themselves and their money. They will be proud and boastful sneering at God. Disobedient to their parents ungrateful to them and thoroughly bad. V-3 they will be hardheaded and never give in to others. They will be constant liars and trouble makers and will think nothing of immorality. They will be rough and crude and sneer at those who try to be good. V-4 They will destroy their friends and they will be hotheaded puffed up with pride and prefer good times to worshiping God. (They will go to church) but they won't really believe anything they hear. Don't be taken in by people like this. Boy these verses hit the nail right on the head for these times in our lives. I hope you can see variations and the way this world is going today. There are many other verses in the Bible that goes along with today's world.

Folks when these times get so hard we can hardly stand it don't just say well God will take hard times away from me. Maybe so or maybe not, probably not. But God has not promised to take them away. But he has promised to go through them with you and be right by your side or close as the words in your mouth. Listen to this verse.(John 17:15-20) I'm not asking you to take them (Christians) out of the world but to keep them safe from Satan's power. V-16 they are not part of this world any more than I am. V-17 But make them pure and holy through teaching them your words of truth. V-18 as you sent me into the world I am sending them into the world. V-19 I consider myself (meet their need) for their growth in truth and holiness. V-20 I am not praying for them alone but also for future believers who will come to me because of their Testimony. This is a prayer from Jesus to his Father God for all disciples even unto this day.

Folks we have to understand just because we are converted that everything is always going to be nice and rosy the rest of our lives' no it is not. Bad things happen to us at times but if we keep the Love of God in our Hearts and keep a good attitude every thing will work out in the end. I have had a lot of bad things happen to me in 38 years but never not one thing didn't work out in the end. Sometimes I thought it wouldn't work out right but they always did. You see my time for things to work out was (not) God's time. Our biggest problem in this area is our patience. We have to have patience and believe in our heart that God is working it out in his time.

I have found out that most of the time it was all my fault that I was in the fix I was in. By not listening to that still small voice or being hardheaded. I would look back in my life and see things he brought me through and think well he didn't let me down back then and why should he let me down now. Folks I look back at my life and I can say I am a Blessed man in all areas and it was not because I have been so good but I have been so forgiven and all the mistakes I have made he still loves me.

None of us are perfect but if we carry this God Kind of Love in our hearts we are forgiven. This is what Jesus went to the Cross for so he can forgive us when we make a mistake. This does not give us a license to sin or make mistakes. We are going to make mistakes as we go through life but we have someone to forgive us and make everything alright if we do our best and repent and ask for forgiveness. If we don't ask for it we won't get it. God will not force us to get this Forgiveness. Wehave to be just like a baby when we fall we just get up ask forgiveness and keep trying to do better. We have to forgive others the same way that God forgave us and forget it and put it in the sea of forgetfulness. We have to do this Forgiveness and forget thing from our heart. In our head it won't be forgotten but from our heart will be that God Kind of Love for them.

We have to pray and ask God for help to do these things This is the way God forgives us he puts them in the sea of forgetfulness. Forgiveness is one of the biggest downfalls in most of Christians lives. They say I forgive you but I won't forget. That is not forgiveness from the heart that is from the head If we don't do it the same way God does it, it is not being done at all. All we are doing is blowing smoke and blowing smoke will not keep us under (The Spout Where The Honey Comes Out). And that means out the window goes God's Blessings. And the Blessings are what keeps us going in this life, in these times of trouble and fear.

Encourage to keep believing and inspire us thanking and praising God for his goodness and they help build our Faith up. (Hebrew 10:39&39) says those whose Faith has made them good in God's sight must live by Faith trusting in everything. Otherwise if they shrink back God will have no pleasure in them. We have never turned our backs on God and Sealed our Fate, no our Faith in him assures our Souls Salvation.(The Living Bible) You see we have tough decisions to make in this life, sinful or Christian lives. Either side has some tough things to decide. A sinful life you have nothing to look forward to in the far far future, In the God Kind of Life.

If we keep God in our heart and life we have all his Blessings plus Eternal Life that means never again no sickness-no unhappiness, All will be as the Angels of God. (Mark 12:25) For when they shall rise from the Dead they neither marry nor are given in marriage but as are Angels of God which are in Heaven.

This also means we will (not die just pass from this life to the next one). (John 8:51) Verily I say unto you (If) a man (keep my saying he shall never see Death). (John 11:26) And whosoever lives and believeth in me shall never die believeth thou this.

(I Corinth 15:55-56) O Death where is thy (sting) O Grave where is thy (Victory). This body is made of Flesh and Blood, it is going to die but our Spirit which is us is not going to the Sting of Death. We (our Spirit) are going to become a Spiritual being like Jesus and where he is at. We will be there to. I think I talked a little about this subject earlier in this book. Sorry but this just came to me to write it. Maybe it is for someone special I don't know, I just don't want to disobey God. I am just trying to write what's in my heart. Things come to me at times and seem so real. I just got to be very very careful cause the enemy is so slick he might try to get me to write something that God doesn't want me to write. We read that in Matthew 5:45 God sends rain on the just and unjust. This is where our Free Will comes in. We have free will to choose to do what we want to. God will not force us to do anything even accept his Blessings. We have to want them and give God the okay and accept them of our own free will. God is not a dictator.

Let's talk a little about why we are here on earth. Did you ever think, what am I doing here, why did God allow me to be born, what is my purpose in this place called Earth. There must be some kind of a destiny for me. My thoughts on this are from studying the Bible. God had created Earth for his High Ark Angel Lucifer son of the morning Isaiah 14th chapter. Ezekiel 28th chapter and then Lucifer started to sin and the father said to his son Jesus let us make man in our image and after our likeness. Just think about that for a little while, isn't that something to think about We all look like God and have his likeness (resemblance-portrait- guise). Boy if you want to know what God looks like just look in a full size mirror, that's what he looks like.

To know this in our hearts we ought to shout like they do at these ball games from the house tops. The reason "I think" that Jesus did this was to have someone to have a personal one on one relationship with, someone he could give all his Blessing to and share his thoughts with and talk to day by day. But that all fell apart in the Garden with Adam and Eve. But I think God knew this was all that's going to happen even before it really happened, Because I think he had a plan for man and woman and also for Satan (Lucifer). Did you ever think about this, we are the only living thing that can worship God. Now up to this point I don't have any Bible to back up what I think, just reading between the lines.

Now God does have a purpose for all of us living on Earth. God's plan has always been to adopt us into his own family. I believe God had a plan for things to go the way everything has went for the last seven thousand years. I think he wanted people to accept the adoption by their Free Will. God wants us to be closer than our spouses or children to him. We were predestined by God from (before time as we know it). He wants us to be just like his son Jesus and we will be to if we keep The God Kind of Love in our Hearts. You see we were made to become like God. (Romans 8:29) For those God foreknew he also (predestined) to be Conformed to the likeness of his son (Jesus) that he might be first among many brothers .

God knew what he was doing from the very beginning, he decided from the outset to "shape the lives" of those who love him along the same lines as the life of his son. We see the original and intended shape of our lives there in him. We don't see how this can be now. But when Christ comes again we will know this time because we will be just like him because we will see him as he really is. God foreknew just what we would be right now. Sooner or later we will do good in our heart unless we "will" not do so. It is always up to us what we make of our lives. We will serve God's purpose for our lives (If) we choose so to do. Because Eternity he has planted in our heart. It is all up to us, it is our choice Our Free Will Eccl 3:11.

(Eph 1:10) This is his purpose or our purpose in Life that when the time is ripe he will gather us all together to be with him in Christ forever and ever and ever. (Isaiah 59:2) Our Iniquities have separated us from God and our sin has hidden his face from us. This life is just preparation for our new life in Eternity where there is no ending of time, no more getting old. Also our purpose is to learn all we can learn about God and then tell the good news to others. God sent his son Jesus to live a life just like we live so he could experience the Kind of Life that we have to live and then take all the things that we have to experience upon himself and die on a cruel Cross so we could be forgiven of the wrong things that we do. So we could live under the New Covenant. Jesus came to save that which was lost by Adam and Eve, Fellowship with God. Jesus said I come to give us Life and Life more abundantly (John 10:10).

The Romans cross is the Cruelest Death that could be administered. I have a tape that's called "that cruel and afford cross". To listen to this tape makes my hair stand up. Jesus said in (Mark 16:15) You go into all the world and preach or teach the Good News to Everyone Everywhere this was Jesus mission in the world. Read about it in Matthew-Mark-Luke-John and he gave us this same mission. But we have to learn about having to do it and experience it ourselves first. And then as his children we are the only way to keep this mission going and he promises us he will be with us every step of the way. But the Bible says (the Husbandman must first be partakers of the fruit) (II Timothy 2:6) The Husbandman that labored must be first partaker of the Fruit.

Folks there is a lot of things we have to go through and have to do that we don't understand why. But they might be for someone else's help. Have anyone ever said something to you and you get thinking about what they said and has helped you in something you were going through. Maybe not nothing big but small but still helped you anyway. I have said before God will use (anything or anybody) he can to get done what he wants done.

And in the end he can also make you to understand why you go through things.

When you ask God for answers to something and he answers in his time his answer will always be for more than one thing. "I think" sometimes he holds up our answer for awhile knowing we need other answers later on. So he waits and gives them all at once (just my thoughts). The word teaches us that if we (keep The God Kind of Love) in our hearts (Spirit) we will be happy and prosper and be in health as our "Soul" prospers (3 John 1:2) This is the words of God and we have to obey or pay the cost. Listen to this (I Samuel 15-16) The Lord told Samuel to say to Saul the King; when thou (you) was little in(your) own sight was thou not made the head of the tribe of Israel and the Lord anointed thee King over Israel and he sent thee on a journey, go and utterly destroy the sinners the Amalekites and fight against until they be consumed, wherefore then didn't thou not obey the voice of the Lord. But didn't fly upon the spoil and did Evil in the Sight of the Lord. And Saul said to Samuel yes I have obeyed the voice of the Lord and have gone the way witch the Lord sent me and have brought Agag the King of Amalek and have utterly destroyed the Amalekites. But the (people took of the Spoil Sheep and oxen the chief of things which (should have been utterly destroyed) took them to sacrifice unto the Lord thy God in Gilgal and Samuel said (has) the Lord great delight in Burnt offerings and sacrifices (as in obeying the Voice of the Lord). Behold to (Obey is better than sacrifice) and to hearken then the fat of rams. For (Rebellion is as the Sin of Witchcraft) and (stubbornness is as iniquity and idolatry).

If we want to stay (under the Spout Where The Honey Flows Out) we have to obey the words (Bible) of the Lord or pay the price. Well now we see Saul forgot where he came from. Forgot all the Blessings God gave him when he made him King. He had all of Israel and every thing in it at his disposal but he was still selfish for something that God had said to destroy everything that walked, The Bible says be satisfied with what you get and God will give you more (Hebrews 13:5) Let your conversation be without covetousness and be content with such things as you have. For he has said I will never leave you or forsake you. Philippians 4:11-Not that I speak in respect of want for I have learned in whatsoever state I am, therewith to be content. Also (Mark 11:23&24&25&26) Be sure to read (Verse 25&26) very important things have to do. Some will say oh I have tried to do this but it does not work. The problem is that there is so much other stuff on our mind that we are really not believing what we are reading. We start out right but cannot focus on what we are trying to believe. Once our mind is on God, I mentioned later it is on something else. This is the enemy doing this to our mind. It is hard to focus on one thing at a time for any length of time in today's world. To have these prayers answered we have to Eat Sleep and Drink God all the time and to do this we have to pray and worship God 24:7 I have this problem all the time while I'm writing this book. God can be pouring things into my mind to write down one minute and the next minute my mind is as blank as a sheet of paper. I have to stop and get my bearings and sometimes it takes days to get me back on track. I don't know about you but I'm learning a lot by just writing this book.

In today's society it is hard to live a life of praise and worship because the enemy has put so much junk and things in our everyday lives to keep us and our minds so packed with do this and do that all day. And when night time comes we are so tired we can't do anything. But greater is he that is in us than the enemy that is in the world. If we can just keep Jesus in front 24-7 he will work it out for us. We can't give up we have to keep right on going and say to the world, we don't have time for you. We are going someplace; don't look right or left but straight ahead. (Don't ever forget where you came from). If he brought you out of a pit he can finish what he started in you if you want him to. There will be times that you will think well I've lost God. No that's the enemy telling you that. Don't accept that he is a liar and the father of lies. Just keep on praying it's the key to success in God. You may think God is not there but he is always as close as the words in your mouth. He will never leave or forsake you. Take my word for it I'm a living example. The Bible says as the days of Sodom and Gomorrah so will be the coming of the Lord.

I read the newspaper every day and watch the news channel on TV and see all the things that are happening and I think I can see the enemy in so many of the things that are happening around the world, that I can see a lot of Sodom and Gomorrah in the world today. I see things that I thought I would never see out in the open fifty years ago. I believe it's the fulfillment of the Bible (II Timothy 3:1 thru 9). lets read this in the living Bible.

You may as well know that's to timely. That in the last days it is going to be very different to be a Christian. For people will love only themselves and their money. They will be proud and boastful sneering at God, disobedient to their parents, ungrateful to them and thoroughly bad. They will be hardheaded and never give in to others. They will be constant liars and troublemakers and will think nothing of immortality. They will be rough and cruel and sneer at those that try to be good. They will betray their friends. They will be hotheaded puffed up with pride and prefer good times to Worshiping God. They will go to church but they really won't believe anything they hear. Don't be taken in by people like that. They are the kind who craftily sneak into other peoples homes and make friendship with folks and teach them their new doctrine. These folks are (forever learning but never able to come to the knowledge of the truth).

These are the kind of people that believe everything the preacher says and never check it out with the Word. They don't know the truth because they don't study the Bible to know whether he is misinformed or plain out lying. If you don't see what is happening in the world today you had better get in the Word and be a doer of the Word and not just a hearer of the Word. And don't play around with God he will only be first in our lives, not second. The things that are happening today that we see on TV and in the news papers are the things that started to happen in Sodom and Gomorrah and led to the fall of that Great City. God will only take so much Sin. Read about this Great City (Genesis 18&19).

This country was founded on God and now people's money and power are taking God out of this country little by little. It's going just to be like Paul The Apostil told (Timothy 3:1).

Folks it's coming as sure as 2+2=4. The power people of this world have been trying to completely control every human being in this world and sooner or later they will. They have been trying this since World War II.

Folks we had better wake up to what is going on around us today. Who are we going to believe (The Word of God) or the things we see going on in the world. I hear people say, oh I can't watch that stuff on TV and read it in the papers, it gets to me. Well the Bible says (watch and pray). Why does it say that? If you are driving down the road at 50 mph why does that sign ahead of you say caution bad curve 20mph (safe speed). What is it trying to tell you? If you don't listen you might go down over the bank and get hurt badly. It's the same way with the Bible. It is trying to tell you something to keep you safe when bad times come to your door, and they will sooner or later. So if we don't listen we will surely feel there are some bad times coming, the handwriting is on the wall.

Some people say good times is here to stay, If you don't believe it just look at the housing market, it's booming property has doubled in the last five years. Well folks gasoline is near $3 a gallon. What is going to happen if it keeps on going up? Already it is starting to be a chain reaction, foods going up, deliveries going up. Service of all kind is going up, repair is going up and gas has only gone up a little over a dollar. What's going to happen if gas keeps going up, God forbid. How is old people going to rent their homes people on a small fixed income. How are they going to eat? You can't get a apartment to rent for no less than four or five hundred dollars, now days that means the rent is going to go up too. The government is not going to help if your income is 500 per month, they won't even talk to you. "Now" what if gas goes up to $5 or $6 dollars a gallon, how is a family going to live on $7 or $8 dollars per hour and the minimum wage is only $5.25 per hour now and the government will not raise it up and a lot of people are only making $5.25 per hour now. Folk's the handwriting is on the wall hard times is coming.

The time is coming the only one's that will be living decent will be the rich or the one's that have a personal relationship with Jesus one on one with (The God Kind of Love in their Heart). This is what "I believe" with all my heart and I believe that all I read in the Bible teaches this. We can't even eat the wild animals or even tame ones, they are getting deceased. Folk's perilous times are coming. If we don't want to believe it that doesn't mean its not going to happen. So we had better prepare ourselves just in case I'm right and the perilous times the Bible talks about will come in our age.

Folks lets talk a little about this (Real Love of God) (our relationship with God) and doing our part of that relationship is like watching a news cast on TV and we are real interested in finding out what is going on about a certain thing that's being talked about and someone comes in and starts talking to you. What happens, you have lost part of the program and it's always the most important part and you and you have lost the whole program. Or someone else walks up and starts a conversation with you or the one you were talking to. What happens for me, I just as well turn around and go home because it just broke up everything I was doing and I forgot it all.

I know some people that love God with all their heart and they live in a state of confusion all the time. Now confusion is not from God, It's from the Devil. The Bible says God is not the author of confusion.I Corinthians 14:33 For God is not the author of confusion but of peace as in all churches of the Saints The times has come that it takes 10 to 12 hours a day to make a half decent living, 3 hours around the house after work, 8 hours sleep at night which leaves us 2 to 3 hours to unwind so we can sleep and pray and read. That means the 12 to 15 hours our minds are so wound up in what we are doing we don't think much about God and worshiping him, this ought not to be. God is not pleased with us being that way. He wants us to slow down and be his friend, talk with him more. How would we feel if our children did us this way, not much of a relationship is it. Well we are God's children you know. God understands we have to work and make a living for our family. But he also wants to be in that part of our lives too. He wants to help us make that living but he wants us to teach ourselves to keep that (Love of God in our Hearts) (Spirit) so he can keep flowing that honey out of his Spout for us.

God wants us to have a relationship with him the type that he takes first place in. Everything we do or say he wants us to teach ourselves to look to him for help in every little thing in our lives or in everything that we need help in like misplacing something and five minutes later we cannot find it. This is just a little thing but if we look to him for help he is always there to help us. I have been a mechanic for fifty years, you would not believe some of the crazy things I have done in my shop and had to ask him for help and he has always been there for me. Some people laugh at me when I tell them things like this, but it works for me. Now I have asked him things to do for me and it has taken years for him to answer, but he always does. Time does not mean a thing to him, with him there is no timing. But he knows when it is time to answer and it always works out right. And then sometimes he answers right away, but he only knows the right time. The Bible says there is a time for everything. (Ecclesiastes 3:1-2-3-4-5) To every thing there is a time and season, a time to every purpose under the Heaven. We have to bring ourselves to the point of knowing when the enemy is working on our mind and trying to sidetrack us and get in our mind on stuff. If its on stuff its not on God. When we get to this point we have to pray and God will be here and help us. I have a sign on my pick up and car (Prayer it Works For Me) and it does work.

Folks God wants to have a relationship with us just like he had with his Son Jesus when Jesus was on Earth those 33 years. He wants to be a part of everything we do and say. But he will not force it on us. That's why he gave us the right to choose the path we take. We have to choose to receive this (Love of God in our Hearts) or not choose to have it. This Christian lifestyle is not easy it takes a real man or women to walk the path. But we have to remember the Blessings that go with it. But the Bible says whatsoever a man sows that's something he will reap. (Galatians 5:7-8) be not deceived God is not mocked: for whatsoever a man sows that shall he also Reap. 8- For he that sows to the flesh reap corruption, but he that sows to the Spirit (good) shall of the Spirit reap life everlasting. If you plant an apple tree you are not going to get peaches off that tree.

We have to keep in mind for us to have a personal relationship with God we have to keep our Hearts pure and clean. Now God understands that we can't be perfect, That's why he sent his Son to die for our Sins. But the Bible says, he who knows to do good and doeth it not it is a sin James 4:17. So we know to do good we have the choice. So there are a lot of things we do from day to day that is sin and we don't believe it and because of a pure heart God does not see it. But if we see it we had better be repenting and ask God for help. Matthew 5:8 says God believes those who's hearts are pure for they shall see God.

The way we live shows what is in our Heart. In other words what's in our heart comes out in our conversations and our ways. Can we share our heart with others that might need help without being ashamed of the way we live or taking care of the Blessings that God has given us? You know we have to take care of the things that God gives us in the material or we may not get some of those things anymore. If you give your kid a gift and he throws it away would you get him another one? Think about it.

When gas prices started going up I could hardly go anyplace. When you are on S.S. you don't have much left over after bills are paid. So I asked God for something to run that (a car) was easy on gas because my old truck was only getting 11 to 12 miles to a gallon. I tried everything I could in myself but to no avail. Then after six months or so I gat a little work I could do from a neighbor not knowing why. Then right away within two hours my wife found a little car in the paper for $300. We went and looked at the car it was like new just needed some engine work. I offered the man $150 and he said yes. I bought it paid cash had enough money left over to overhaul the engine myself. Now I have a real nice car 4 cyl. 25 to 35 mpg. It pays to ask God for what you want, put it in his hands and wait for the answer. Keep a pure Heart (God Kind of Love in your Heart) and he will never fail you. God loves us with a never ending love and he wants to bless us more than we can ever dream of if we let him.

Our relationship has to be right with God. We can hide our feelings from people but we sure can't hide them from God No matter where we go or what we do God is there. He sees all and hears all we do and sees all we feel we just can't hide from God. If our relationship is right with God we do not ever have to worry about anything (but staying Under the Spout Where the Honey flows out). The word says cast your worries on him (I Peter 5:7) Don't worry about your everyday needs God already knows all your needs and he will give them to us day by day if you live for him and make him your primary concern. Just talk to him and tell him what you need and he will answer and thank him for all he has done already. After all we were able to get up this morning and still breath after being dead (asleep) all night. That's a miracle in itself. (Matthew 6:25-32-33) also (Matthew 11:28). If we would give as much thought to our relationship with God as we give to our daily lives we would be so much better off. Just think of how much more Love we would have in our Heart for others and how much more Blessings we would have and how much more peace we would have in our lives. About 80% of the world today has no respect for God at all. Just look at the earthquakes and Florida's hurricanes. In 2005 millions and millions have died in those things and some are still dancing in the streets, drinking and shouting and cursing God to his face after he sent his only child Jesus to die on a cruel Cross for them. Because he loved them that much with an everlasting love and all he ever wanted was a good relationship with them and to bless them with untold Blessings. And here we have a bunch of men doing their best to get God completely out of our lives and our country and government just standing by letting them get away with this. Shame on our government after all this country was founded on God. This country had better wake up and vote every man out of office on election day that doesn't have a good relationship with our creator. Or as the Apostle Paul told Timothy there is more perilous times coming, wake up folks.

Folks as the Bible says, as the days of Sodom and Gomorrah was so shall it be in the coming of the Lord (Matthews 24:37). Folks this world is on a fast path to becoming as those days. In (Matthew 25:1-12) There were virgins (all 10) what happened to 5 of them they didn't prepare enough, they came at first ready but they didn't prepare for the long term. It is not the man who runs in the race but it's the man that finishes the race that wins. We have to keep up with our relationship and keep it pure and at Gods feet all the time and let nothing stand in between us and God, I say (Nothing). God will not take second place, he says first or nothing. Anything between us and God is a God to us. We can have a relationship with God that is not pure, there is a difference. Some folks think they can have a relationship with God and do what they want to do through the week and on Sunday do what God wants. Folks that will not work, that's like throwing a glass of water against the wind its coming right back on you. The old saying is true that whatever you put out you take in. In other words if you plant flowers you don't put weed seeds in the ground. We have to have that God Kind of Love in out Hearts. Relationships will not survive without that Kind of Love in our heart. That's what makes pure hearts and without pure hearts regardless of how much we work or do for God we will not get the Blessings that he wants to give us. We can not earn these Blessings by working for God. We have to believe obedience is better than sacrifice. The Bible says we have to read and study the Bible and be a doer of the word not just a reader of this Bible. Now there are some of you out there that want to have a relationship like I am talking about but you say I just can't do this. Well I can remember the time I said the same thing, you can not do it on your own but you can do it with Gods help. God knows you can not do it on your own and he says ask and be sincere in your asking and he will help you.

You can't just start off and do it like right now it takes a little time. But you just refuse to give it up. If you fall out of line just talk to God and ask him to help you and just keep on trying. It's hard to learn just about anything that you haven't done before. But you don't just stop because you're afraid, you just repent and get yourself by the seat of your pants and say we are going to do this by the help of God. Every time you do this it will get easier. Be honest with yourself and don't be afraid to admit you're wrong. God only requires you to put forth your best effort. When you start to build a relationship it takes time and sometimes it's hard to do. It takes a lot of changes on both parties at the same time. Sometimes when we start this process we see some things in our life that we didn't even know was there and sometimes it is something that we don't want to get rid of and this could be a fight on our part. But we desire to have relationships and we know we can't have one unless we get rid of certain things in our life, There is nothing in this world like having the Blessings of God in our life. A good relationship with God is very very rewarding. This kind of a relationship is the most important thing that can happen to us in our lifetime.

Listen to what God has to say in Isaiah 1:18 no matter how deep the stain of your sins I can make you as clean as freshly fallen snow even if you are stained as red as crimson, I can make you as white as wool. But we can't give up if we fall we just keep on keeping on. God will always be there for us. Sometimes it just doesn't feel like it but his promise is he will never leave or forsake us. He is always as close as the words in our mouth. We don't realize how much God loves sometimes we think he is like a dictator and every time we make a mistake he wants to bang us on the head. But this is not true; it is true he does every thing he can to make us walk in love because he knows this is the best way to a happy and prosperous life now and the life to come. He has a destiny for every person if they will let him lead them to that destiny. But he will not force them to do this it is our choice.

Well in closing if you have read this book I pray I have said something to you to encourage you and help you along this life's pathway and to say that there is a better way of life and a happier life.

The Bible says in II Corinthians 12:19 again thank you that we excuse ourselves into you. We speak before God in Christ; but we do all things dearly beloved for your Edifying. Also Romans 12:19 so I hope I have Edified you in this book.

If you would like to try this way of Life you have nothing to loose and the whole world to gain. Thank you for reading this book.

Just Repeat This B.A.S.E. for Your Life

B. Believe that Jesus died on the cross for me and he showed me that he was God by coming back to life. Do you believe this?

a. Accept Gods free forgiveness for my Sins. Do you want to do this?

S. Switch to Gods plan for my life. Are you willing to do that?

E. Express my desire for Christ to be the dictator of my life. Would you like to do that?

Printed in the United States
93604LV00004B/439-480/A

9 781434 316608